Uplands

Uplands

New Poems

· ·

A. R. AMMONS

W · W · NORTON & COMPANY · INC ·

NEW YORK

for Mona and Vida

Contents

Acknowledgments

I thank the editors of the following periodicals for first publishing the poems listed:

Poetry: "Conserving the Magnitude of Uselessness," "If Anything will Level with you Water Will," "The Unifying Principle," "Runoff," "Transaction," "Then One," "Mountain Talk," "Love Song," "Love Song (2)," "Spiel."
The Hudson Review: "Classic," "Further On," "Life in the Boondocks," "Help," "Script," "Guitar Recitativos."
The New York Times: "Impulse," "Mule Song," "Small Song."
Southern Poetry Review: "Snow Log," "Periphery," "Hope's Okay."
Apple: "Clarity," "Virtu."
The Quest: "Offset," "Cascadilla Falls."
Epoch: "Summer Session 1968."
Compass Review: "Apologia pro Vita Sua."
Foxfire: "Laser."
Kumquat: "Body Politic."
NEW: American and Canadian Poetry: "Holly."
Pebble: "Upland."
Stony Brook Poetry Journal: "Needs."
Tri-Quarterly: "Possibility Along a Line of Difference."

I acknowledge with gratitude permission to use the unwitting contributions of my colleagues Barry Adams and Neil Hertz to "Summer Session 1968."
A Guggenheim Fellowship (1966) and the Traveling Fellowship of the American Academy of Arts and Letters (1967) helped

greatly by giving me free time to write this collection.

The poems "Impulse," "Mule Song," and "Small Song" ©
1969 by The New York Times Company. Reprinted by permi
sion. "Guitar Recitativos" has appeared in *Best Poems of 1968* an
in *The American Literary Anthology*.

Uplands

Snow Log

Especially the fallen tree
the snow picks
out in the woods to show:

the snow means nothing by that,
no special emphasis: actually
snow picks nothing out:

but was it a failure, is it,
snow's responsible for
that the brittle upright black

shrubs and small trees
set off what caught the snow
in special light:

or there's some intention
behind the snow snow's too shallow
to reckon with: I take it on myself:

especially the fallen tree
the snow picks
out in the woods to show.

Upland

Certain presuppositions are altered
by height: the inversion to
sky-well a peak
in a desert makes: the welling

from clouds down the boulder fountains:
it is always a
surprise out west there—
the blue ranges loose and aglide

with heat and then come close
on slopes leaning up into green:
a number of other phenomena might
be summoned—

take the Alleghenies for example,
some quality in the air
of summit stones lying free and loose
out among the shrub trees: every

exigency seems prepared for that might
roll, bound, or give flight
to stone: that is, the stones are
prepared: they are round and ready.

Periphery

One day I complained about the periphery
that it was thickets hard to get around in
    or get around for
an older man: it's like keeping charts

of symptoms, every reality a symptom
where the ailment's not nailed down:
    much knowledge, precise enough,
but so multiple it says this man is alive

or isn't: it's like all of a body answering
all of pharmacopoeia, a too
    adequate relationship:
so I complained and said maybe I'd brush

deeper and see what was pushing all this
periphery, so difficult to make any sense
    out of, out:
with me, decision brings its own

hesitation: a symptom, no doubt, but open
and meaningless enough without paradigm:
    but hesitation
can be all right, too: I came on a spruce

thicket full of elk, gushy snow-weed,
nine species of lichen, four pure white
   rocks and
several swatches of verbena near bloom.

Clarity

After the event the rockslide
realized,
in a still diversity of completion,
grain and fissure,
declivity
&
force of upheaval,
whether rain slippage,
ice crawl, root
explosion or
stream erosive undercut:

well I said it is a pity:
one swath of sight will never
be the same: nonetheless,
this
shambles has
relieved a bind, a taut of twist,
revealing streaks &
scores of knowledge
now obvious and quiet.

Classic

I sat by a stream in a
perfect—except for willows—
emptiness
and the mountain that
was around,

scraggly with brush &
rock
said
I see you're scribbling again:

accustomed to mountains,
their cumbersome intrusions,
I said

well, yes, but in a fashion very
like the water here
uncapturable and vanishing:

but that
said the mountain does not
excuse the stance
or diction

and next if you're not careful
you'll be
arriving at ways
water survives its motions.

Conserving the Magnitude
of Uselessness

Spits of glitter in lowgrade ore,
precious stones too poorly surrounded for harvest,
to all things not worth the work
of having,

brush oak on a sharp slope, for example,
the balk tonnage of woods-lodged boulders,
the irreparable desert,
drowned river mouths, lost shores where

the winged and light-footed go,
take creosote bush that possesses
ground nothing else will have,
to all things and for all things

crusty or billowy with indifference,
for example, incalculable, irremovable water
or fluvio-glacial deposits
larch or dwarf aspen in the least breeze sometimes shiver in—

suddenly the salvation of waste betides,
the peerlessly unsettled seas that shape the continents,
take the gales wasting and in waste over
Antarctica and the sundry high shoals of ice,

for the inexcusable (the worthless abundant) the
merely tiresome, the obviously unimprovable,
to these and for these and for their undiminishment
the poets will yelp and hoot forever

probably,
rank as weeds themselves and just as abandoned:
nothing useful is of lasting value:
dry wind only is still talking among the oldest stones.

If Anything Will Level
with You Water Will

Streams shed out of mountains in a white rust
(such the abomination of height)
slow then into upland basins or high marsh

and slowing drop loose composed figurations
on big river bottoms
or give the first upward turn from plains:

that's for modern streams: if sediment's
lithified it
may have to be considered ancient, the result of

a pressing, perhaps lengthy, induration:
old streams from which the water's
vanished are interesting, I mean that

kind of tale,
water, like spirit, jostling hard stuff around
to make speech into one of its realest expressions:

water certainly is interesting (as is spirit) and
small rock, a glacial silt, just as much so:
but most pleasurable (magma & migma) is

rock itself in a bound slurp or spill
or overthrust into very recent times:
there waterlike stone, those heated seekings &

goings, cools to exact concentration, I
mean the telling is unmediated:
the present allows the reading of much

old material: but none of it need be read:
it says itself (and
said itself) so to speak perfectly in itself.

The Unifying Principle

Ramshackles, archipelagoes, loose constellations
are less fierce, subsidiary centers, with the
attenuations of interstices, roughing the salience,

jarring the outbreak of too insistent commonalty:
a board, for example, not surrendering the rectitude
of its corners, the island of the oaks an

admonishment to pines, underfigurings (as of the Bear)
that take identity on: this motion is against
the grinding oneness of seas, hallows distinction

into the specific: but less lovely, too, for how
is the mass to be amassed, by what sanction
neighbor touch neighbor, island bear resemblance,

how are distinction's hard lines to be dissolved
(and preserved): what may all the people turn to,
the old letters, the shaped, characteristic peak

generations of minds have deflected and kept:
a particular tread that sometimes unweaves, taking
more shape on, into dance: much must be

tolerated as out of timbre, out of step, as being not
in its time or mood (the hiatus of the unconcerned)
and much room provided for the wretched to find caves

to ponder way off in: what then can lift the people
and only when they choose to rise or what can make
them want to rise, though business prevents: the

unifying principle will be a
phrase shared, an old cedar long known, general
wind-shapes in a usual sand: those objects single,

single enough to be uninterfering, multiple by
the piling on of shared sight, touch, saying:
when it's found the people live the small wraths of ease.

Runoff

By the highway the stream downslope
could hardly clear itself
through rubbish and slime but by

that resistance gained a cutting
depth equal to its breadth
and so had means to muscle into

ripples and spill over angled
shelves:
and so went on down in a long

curve, responsively slow to the
sizable ridge it
tended

and farther on down, quiet and clear,
never tipping enough to break sound,
slowed into marshy landrise and burst

into a bog of lupine and mirrored:
that was a place! what a place!
the soggy small marsh, nutgrass and swordweed!

Transaction

I attended the burial of all my rosy feelings:
I performed the rites, simple and decisive:
the long box took the spilling of gray ground in
with little evidence of note: I traded slow

work for the usual grief: the services were private:
there was little cause for show, though no cause not
to show: it went indifferently, with an appropriate
gravity and lack of noise: the ceremonies of the self

seem always to occur at a distance from the ruins of men
where there is nothing really much to expect, no arms,
no embraces: the day was all right: certain occasions
outweigh the weather: the woods just to the left

were average woods: well, I turned around finally from
the process, the surface smoothed into a kind of seal,
and tried to notice what might be thought to remain:
everything was there, the sun, the breeze, the woods

(as I said), the little mound of troublesome tufts of
grass: but the trees were upright shadows, the breeze
was as against a shade, the woods stirred gray
as deep water: I looked around for what was left,

the tools, and took them up and went away, leaving
all my treasures where they might never again disturb
me, increase or craze: decision quietens:
shadows are bodiless shapes, yet they have a song.

Then One

When the circumstance takes
on a salience, as a

crushing pressure, then one,
addled by the possible closures,

the tangles that might
snap taut in a loop

or other unfigurable construct,
then one

pores on drift-logs far at sea
where room can wear drifts out

winds change
and few places show one can't

embark
from and then one thinks finally

with tight appreciation
of nothingness

or if not that far of
things that loosen or come apart.

Further On

Up this high and far north
it's shale and woodsless snow:
small willows and alder brush

mark out melt streams on the
opposite slope and the wind talks
as much as it can before freeze

takes the gleeful, glimmering
tongues away: whips and sticks
will scream and screech then

all winter over the deaf heights,
the wind lifting its saying out
to the essential yell of the

lost and gone: it's summer now:
elk graze the high meadows:
marshgrass heads high as a moose's

ears: lichen, a wintery weed,
fills out for the brittle sleep:
waterbirds plunder the shallows.

Hope's Okay

The undergrowth's a conveyance of butterflies
(flusters of clustering) so buoyant and delightful,
filling into a floating impression, diversity's
diversion breaking out into under-piny seas
point by point to the mind's nodes and needs:

let's see, though, said the fire through the undergrowth,
what all this makes into, what difference can
survive it:

                 so I waded through the puffy disgust
and could not help feeling despair of
many a gray, smoke-worming twig, scaly as if alive:

much that was here I said is lost and if I stoop
to ask bright thoughts of roots
do not think I ask for better than was here
or that hope with me rises one leaf higher than
the former growth (higher to an ashless fire) or
that despair came any closer than ash to being total.

Life in the Boondocks

Untouched grandeur in the hinterlands:
large-lobed ladies laughing in brook
water, a clear, scrubbed ruddiness lofted

to cones and conifers: frost blurs
the morning elk there and squirrels
chitter with the dawn, numb seed: clarity,

the eagle dips into scary nothingness,
off a bluff over canyon heights: trout
plunder their way up, thrashing the shallows

white: ladies come out in the gold-true sun
and loll easy as white boulders
in the immediate radiance by wind-chilling

streams: I have been there so
often, so often and held the women, squeezed,
tickled, nuzzled their rose-paint luxury:

so many afternoons listened to the rocky
drone of bees over spring-water weed-bloom,
snow-water violets, and distant moss turf.

Spiel

    I feel sure you will be pleased
with our product: it is
a coil spring comes wintrily into
   as house plants
react first to the longer light:

             but begin all
enterprise with celebration: measures
on the sand by
fluttering rush, sail, heart spun in
a resonance between
departure, grief and adventure of
   change, the hurry and detail,
sudden calamity
of shoving off, moorless into a hunk of
time that may
round back to greet its other edge:
may:

(nothing is so phony as an incomplete
   obscurity—it needs spelling
   into its deepest outing,
   surrounding into its biggest bulging:
   when it gets aglitter
   it grows black: what to make of a

hinted thing
where the mind's not traveled
but a botch: but spelled out any
spiel can pick enough surfage up
to drum a sea loose)

I just ate a green banana: it is in
me now mushed and gushy: there is
nothing small enough to conjure clarity with:

take the bathroom spider wintered thin:
so thin
bleached out against walls
life seems in him a brown taint that
lacking might make him water or crisp:
he spun an open-ended house
(safety, closed up to perfection,
        traps, he knows)
                in the ceilingwall sharp
angle:

        (well then I will take a mere
suasion!
a drift
as of earth into light, the chorus
dancing to the right,
left, a multimedial parlance:
well I will take just the angle
the waves come out of the sea, say,
the way they break down their length
in a continuous moving roar:
        I don't care how many drops of

water there are
or how totally they are water or how
the ocean is nothing (figuratively
speaking) else: I identify waves,
they have an
action, many actions: I've seen them
come straight in, crest first in
the middle, break outward both ways
and leave behind
a pyramid of foam: I've never
seen a drop of water do that:)

at night he rides down to the white
sink
and hums in a drop of water's
uptight edge: I try to think
of what he eats
so winter skinny, such a bugless
winter: maybe those tiny book lice
leave learning
scoot ceilings sometimes and suffer
the usual
confrontation with reality:
or I think dandruff scales soaked in
droplets
drift dripping proteins loose that
drunk skirl spiders into hallelujahs
  of darkening:

from the state of distress a pill can
remove you: meanwhile the blue
spruce
is perilously unaffected:

                    it's monsterless here:
the
bayberry in a green sweep, breeze
lively:
indifferent as lace:

swipes, swatches, smears, luminous
samplers: what is

the existence in the argument of what
the argument
is about: precise but unspecified,
hunted out, turned from, disguised,
brunted:

                    order, strict,
                       is the shadow of flight:
I mean because of the lusterless
structure
the wing has rein: fact
is the port of
extreme navigation:

where footprints
disappear at the edge of melting snow
hesitation breaks mindfully into itself:

            the fairgrounds

(hill meadows, aslant
    triangular sweepclosings of heights,
    scrub fringes, yangs of woods,

lovely sumac and sassafras, golden
clumps of grass
rising to a wind line, commas,
the pheasant's tail, long,
perfect for disappearance in
winter weeds, clumpy printwork
of rabbits
over hedge-kept floats of snow. . .

I don't know what all there is
but there's more than plenty and
that's just it there's too much
except for, there'd be too much
except for the outgrowth of soothing
hills)

   sporting goods

nip and tuck
scoops
scopes
scrimps &
scroungings

Guitar Recitativos

1

I know you love me, baby
I know it by the way you carry on around here certain times
of the day and night
I can make the distinction between the willing and the
unrefusable
That's not what I'm talking about
That's not what I need
What I mean is could you just peel me a few of those grapes
over there
I want to lie here cool and accumulate
Oh say about half a bunch
That's what I need—flick out those little seed—
Just drop them in here one at a time
I'm not going anyplace, baby, not today
Relax—sneak the skin off a few of those grapes for me, will you?

2

Baby, you been stomping round on my toes so long
they breaking out in black and blue hyacinths,
well-knit forget-me-nots
Geraniums are flopping out over the tops of my shoes
tendril leaves coming out along the edges of my shoelaces

Gladioli are steering out of the small of my back
strumming those cool stalks up my spine
Zinnias radiating from the crock of my neck
and petunias swinging down bells from my earlobes
All this stomping around on me you been doing, baby,
I'm gonna break out in a colorful reaction
I'm gonna wade right through you
with the thorns of all these big red roses

3

I'm tired of the you-and-me thing
I am for more research into the nature of the amorous bond
the discovery of catalysts for speeding-up, wearing out,
     and getting it over with
or for slowing it down to allow long intervals of looseness

Baby, there are times when the mixture becomes immiscible
and other times we get so stirred up I can't tell
whether I'm you or me
and then I have this fear of a surprising reaction in which
we both turn into something else

powdery or gaseous or slightly metallic
What I mean is this whole relationship is, lacking further
knowledge, risky: while there's still time, why
don't you get yourself together and I'll

get myself together and then we'll sort of shy out
of each other's gravitational field, unstring the
electromagnetism, and then sort of just drop this
whole orientation, baby

4

I can tell you what I think of your beauty, baby,
you have it, it's keen and fast, there's this
glittery sword whipping about your head all day
and, baby, you make people snap—you condescend

and a surprised little heart splatters or you turn your
cold head away and a tiny freeze kills a few
cells in some man's brain—I mean, baby, you
may be kind but your beauty, sweetie, is such

many a man would run himself through for
hating your guts every minute that he died for you

5

You come in and I turn on:
freon purrs and the
refrigerator breaks out with hives of ice:
the Westinghouse portable electric fan flushes
my papers all over the room:
the waffle-iron whacks down sizzling imaginary waffles:
one paper glues itself and billows to the back of the fan,
my nerves nervous as newspapers:

I tell you, you are a walking calamity
and when you sit down there is hardly less activity:
the alarm clock breaks out raging its held cry
and the oven in the kitchen sets itself for broil:

I mean the gas-jet in the incinerator bloops on
and, frankly, the mechanisms in my legs—I hope you
   never find out—jerk:
Oh, beauty, beauty is so disturbingly nice.

Laser

An image comes
and the mind's light, confused
as that on surf
or ocean shelves,
gathers up,
parallelizes, focuses
and in a rigid beam illuminates the image:

the head seeks in itself
fragments of left-over light
to cast a new
direction,
any direction,
to strike and fix
a random, contradicting image:

but any found image falls
back to darkness or
the lesser beams splinter and
go out:
the mind tries to
dream of diversity, of mountain
rapids shattered with sound and light,

of wind fracturing brush or
bursting out of order against a mountain
range: but the focused beam
folds all energy in:
the image glares filling all space:
the head falls and
hangs and cannot wake itself.

Virtu

Make a motion
the wind said and
the mountain
strained hard
but

couldn't
even quiver:

so the wind curved and shook the poplars:
a slope
pebble loosened
and struck

down sharp goings:

the mountain
stunned at being
moved nearly
broke with grief

and the wind
whirled up the valley
over the stream

and trees
utterly unlost
in emptiness.

Choice

Idling through the mean space dozing,
blurred by indirection, I came upon a
stairwell and steadied a moment to
think against the stem:
upward turned golden steps
and downward dark steps entered the dark:

unused to other than even ground I
spurned the airless heights though bright
and the rigor to lift an immaterial soul
and sank
sliding in a smooth rail whirl and fell
asleep in the inundating dark
but waking said god abhors me
but went on down obeying at least
the universal law of gravity:

millenniums later waking in a lightened air
I shivered in high purity
and still descending grappled with
the god that
rolls up circles of our linear
sight in crippling disciplines
tighter than any climb.

Body Politic

Out for stars he
took some
down
and we all
wondered if he might be
damned to such sinister
& successful enterprise:
we took and
unfolded him: he
turned out
pliant and warm
& messy in
some minor way: then, not
having come to
much we
lit into his stars which
declaring nothing dark
held white and high
and brought us down.

Apologia pro Vita Sua

I started picking up the stones
throwing them into one place
and by sunrise I was going far away
for the large ones
always turning to see never lost
the cairn's height
lengthening my radial reach:

the sun watched with deep concentration
and the heap through the hours grew
and became by nightfall
distinguishable from all the miles around
of slate and sand:

during the night the wind falling
turned earthward its lofty freedom and speed
and the sharp blistering sound muffled
toward dawn and the blanket was
drawn up over a breathless face:

even so you can see in full dawn
the ground there lifts
a foreign thing desertless in origin.

Offset

Losing information he
rose gaining
view
till at total
loss gain was
extreme:
extreme & invisible:
the eye
seeing nothing
lost its
separation:
self-song
(that is a mere motion)
fanned out
into failing swirls
slowed &
became continuum.

Mountain Talk

I was going along a dusty highroad
when the mountain
across the way
turned me to its silence:
oh I said how come
I don't know your
massive symmetry and rest:
nevertheless, said the mountain,
would you want
to be
lodged here with
a changeless prospect, risen
to an unalterable view:
so I went on
counting my numberless fingers.

Impulse

If a rock on the slope
loosens tonight
will it be because
rain's
unearthed another grain
or a root
arched for room
and
will a tree or rock
be right
there, or two rocks or trees,
to hold the
flashed decision back?

Needs

I want something suited to my special needs
I want chrome hubcaps, pin-on attachments
and year round use year after year
I want a workhorse with smooth uniform cut,
dozer blade and snow blade & deluxe steering
wheel
I want something to mow, throw snow, tow
and sow with
I want precision reel blades
I want a console styled dashboard
I want an easy spintype recoil starter
I want combination bevel and spur gears, 14
gauge stamped steel housing and
washable foam element air cleaner
I want a pivoting front axle and extrawide
turf tires
I want an inch of foam rubber inside a vinyl
covering
and especially if it's not too much, if I
can deserve it, even if I can't pay for it
I want to mow while riding.

Help

From the inlet
surf a father
pulls in a crab—
a wonderful machinery
but
not a fish: kicks
it off the line &
up the beach
where three daughters
and two sons take
turns bringing cups
of water
to keep alive, to
watch work, the sanded
& disjeweled.

Love Song

Like the hills under dusk you
fall away from the light:
you deepen: the green
light darkens
and you are nearly lost:
only so much light as
stars keep
manifests your face:
the total night in
myself raves
for the light along your lips.

Love Song (2)

Rings of birch bark
stand in the woods
still circling the nearly
vanished log: after
we go to pass
through log and star
this white song will
hug us together in the
woods of some lover's head.

Mule Song

Silver will lie where she lies
sun-out, whatever turning the world does,
longeared in her ashen, earless,
floating world:
indifferent to sores and greenage colic,
where oats need not
come to,
bleached by crystals of her trembling time:
beyond all brunt of seasons, blind
forever to all blinds,
inhabited by
brooks still she may wraith over broken
fields after winter
or roll in the rye-green fields:
old mule, no defense but a mule's against
disease, large-ribbed,
flat-toothed, sold to a stranger, shot by a
stranger's hand,
not my hand she nuzzled the seasoning-salt from.

Script

The blackbird takes out
from the thicket down there
uphill toward
the house, shoots
through a vacancy in the
elm tree & bolts
over the house:
some circling leaves waving
record
size, direction, and speed.

Holly

The hollybush flowers
small whites (become of
course berries)
four tiny petals
turned
back and four
anthers stuck out:
the pistil low &
honey-high:
wasp-bees (those small
wasps or
bees) come around
with a glee too
fine to hear: when
the wind dies
at dusk, silence,
unaffronted,
puts a robe
slightly thinner
than sight over
all the flowers
so darkness &
the terrible stars
will not hurt them.

Small Song

The reeds give
way to the

wind and give
the wind away

Possibility Along
a Line of Difference

At the crustal
discontinuity
I went down and
walked
on the gravel bottom,
head below gully rims

tufted with
clumpgrass and
through-free roots:
prairie flatness crazed
by that difference,
I grew

excited with
the stream's image left
in dust
and farther down
in confined rambling
I

found a puddle
green, iridescent

with a visitation of daub-singing wasps,
sat down and watched
tilted shadow untilting
fill the trough,

imagined cloudbursts
and
scattered pillars of rain,
buffalo at night routed
by lightning,
leaping,

falling back,
wobble-kneed calves
tumbling, gully-caught;
coyote, crisp-footed
on the gravel,
loping up the difference.

Cascadilla Falls

I went down by Cascadilla
Falls this
evening, the
stream below the falls,
and picked up a
handsized stone
kidney-shaped, testicular, and

thought all its motions into it,
the 800 mph earth spin,
the 190-million-mile yearly
displacement around the sun,
the overriding
grand
haul

of the galaxy with the 30,000
mph of where
the sun's going:
thought all the interweaving
motions
into myself: dropped

the stone to dead rest:
the stream from other motions

broke
rushing over it:
shelterless,
I turned

to the sky and stood still:
oh
I do
not know where I am going
that I can live my life
by this single creek.

Summer Session 1968

Saliences are humming bee paths
in & out around
here, continuous if
unpredictable: they
hang the air with cotton
candy
and make a neighborhood:

we set out four tomato plants a while
ago: good soil
where a row of winter-used cut wood was:
I've been out several times to see
but coming dark hinders me,
forcing faith up which
must
spindly as high walloping
weeds
outlast the night:

earlier came a shower so
skinny
not a coil spring in the glass pond
rang the periphery, for a minute:

walking home from class:
dogs yurping

out from hedge tunnels,
jerking to snazzy, skidding halts,
an outrage about the legs,
hairy explosion with
central, floating teeth:
I hope snitching hairy little
worms
will thread their eyelids and distending close off
the eyeballs of flagrant sight the way
summer closed up the
hedges to fill
us with surprises:

in my yard's more wordage than I
can read:
the jaybird gives a shit:
the earthworm hoe-split bleeds
against a damp black clump:

the problem is
how
to keep shape and flow:

the day's died
& can't be re-made:
in the dusk I can't recover
the goldenbodied fly
that waited on a sunfield leaf:

well I can't recover the light:
in my head—on the
inside frontal wall—the fly waits

and then, as he did, darts upward at an
air-hung companion:

ghosts remain, essences out-skinnying
light: essences
perceiving ghosts skinny skinny
percipients:
reverence, which one cannot
withhold, is
laid on lightly, with terror—as if
one were holding a dandelion back
into the sun:

all these shapes my bones
answer to
are going to go on
consuming, the flowers, venations, vines,
the roots that know their
way,
going to go on taking down and
re-designing, are going to go on
stridently
with bunchers & shears
devouring sundry mud, flesh: but their
own shapes will, as will all shapes, break
but will with all
others
cast design ahead where possible, hold
figuration in the cast seed:
shape & flow:
we must not feel hostile:

the most perfect nothingness affords
the widest play,
the most perfect meaninglessness:
look up at dusk and see
the bead fuzzy-buzzy bug
no darker than mist:
couldn't get along
at all except against infinity:
swallow, bat dine
in a rush—
never know what hit him
nothing hit him sent him to nothing:
but the temporary marvels!—
getting along against. . . .
take it from there:

(to slink and dream with the interior singing
attention of snakes)

prolix as a dream, a stream, sameness
of going
but diverse, colorful, sunlit
glints and glimmerings:
can motion alone then
hold you, strange person:
entertainments of flame and water,
flame in water,
an honorable, ancient flame
removed in high burning: water
no less a metal of interest, subtly
obeying: sit down and be consoled:
the death that reaches toward you has

been spared none:
be enchanted with the shrill hunger
of distant children:
do something:

the boughs ripen:
birds falling out
around here like plums,
rolling around, tilting over, turbulent
somersaults, a wrestling with divinity,
smooth & mostly belly:
the tail's a mean instrument but
feathered
gives poise, as of
contrary knowledges:
the cats frizzling with interest tone
down to pure motion: songs go
such way:
destruction of the world into the
guts: regeneration:
the kill is a restless
matter: but
afterwards the fact's
cool as satiation:

we just had lunch at the picnic table
under the elm: chunks of cantaloupe,
peach slices, blueberries, all cool
colorings in a glass cup: hotdogs &
pepsi:
brilliant replenishment:
icy destructions with the berry

burst, the teeth in a freshet
of cantaloupe juice:
the robin's nest, way out on a pear
limb, nearly
overhangs the table: some
worry, of course, a chirp or two:
distant approaches: above, the yellow
triangles of mouths:

up the stairs you go
up the stairs you go
beddybye &
snoozy snooze
up the stairs you go
ho ho
up the stairs you go

now the lawnmowers of reality are
whirring on the slopes of absent lawns
and sunday is in the world or part
of it: I look across the valley
to the otherside big hills and realize
the whole thing's rolling
tumbling in the smoothest quietest
lunge, our
bristlegreen rockship, our clamorous
house wherein difference bites so
hard hardly
a man will admit the common nickelodean core
where metals twist in
slow drifts of warping
pressure:

nevertheless into raw
space we turn, sun
feeding cosmic drift through,
expelling radiance of cosmic storm,
and we are at an
incredible height going round
something:
in the whole coming and going of man
we may not
get around once:
at certain levels recurrence is not
a bore: we clip an arc:

buttered batter's better bitter:

what do you know:
Western Prong beat Old Dock:
stir up them little wasps and you
have a nest of hornets:

past 2 1
women suffer
unbearably (!)
take bladder irritation: that headachy
backachy feeling:
that burning stitching itching gives them
the weewee's, makes them need
fast relaxing comfort: what women go
through
to make or lose a buck: in those
ample haunches
greased with sheer illumination's light

is a mess of bacterial bloomers: it's
merciful to lust the eye's
small-blind: cultures from average nipples:
knowledge is lovely
but some of it shivers
into the blood stream
and undermines the
requirements of the moment: but
desire spills antiseptic gold celluloid
sheathes o'erall
and pours pellucid lubricants
down the drains of microfloral
habitations:
the clitoris rises above
surmountings, backs off, and
takes a testy peck or so:

we went to the park & John swung on
the swings and swung:
little children, I told my wife,
these little children, some of them
will live to say two thousand forty
maybe forty-five, fifty:
I said think of it by that time
we, you and I, will have been dead
so long
worms yet will scoff at us:
it makes you think
(twice):
what are
a few vaginal weeds in the teeth
compared with the traipsing gluebellies of

candorous maggots: & other worms,
all their noise:
get down, yes:
enwarm to eradication the carnal
longings: which are short:

what, then, is the organization of the
soul: scrambles to the peak,
squirts off, slumps back: the
long & short of it:

ducks were there, spinning, sputtering
in the glass: popcorn, wiener rolls
floating in the circumstance: but do
they do do underwater:
if a scientist, I'd devise
a test
and count the dropping abstractions off:
a glass tank with top
and a careful observer
could keep that duck in there
till he had to: yes, but the
test's wrong: supposed the observed's
disturbed & would much have
preferred
to go out upon the ground & hunker up on
a hunk of grass:
could turn to billets due
formerly:
following a duck around au naturel
though
could wobble a man's weltanschauung:

scientific objectivity puts
radiance on
duckshit even: we used to save
coop chickenshit for choicest
garden plants:
a powerful ingredient that
through the delicacies of floral
transfiguration
makes tasty gravy:

friend of mine, brilliant
linguist, told me
a Southern Gentleman screwed
himself in the
penis
with a squirrel's
pizzle:
puzzling:
got it hung in there's how everybody
found out:
doctor had to cut it loose:

let approved channels then be your
contemplation
so you will not wind up in a fix
or fuxy fox, feel the fire asphaltic:
do
not go in for strange devices:
pins, strangulations or such:
practices that lead gradually away
from picnic tables,
the trivial fluvial fumes of sunday braziers:

I'm not going to
delay my emergence:
I'm going to plop
a polyp:
I'm going to pupate
pussycoon:
I'm going to shoot for the wings:
I can't tell you how many times with
stalled interior I've
watched the spiders hatch & thrive:
I'm going to
get something off my chest—
incubus or poking heartflipper:
I'm 42:
the rank & file has
o'errucked me & cloddled on:
I'm not going
any longer officially
to delay my emergence:
I want the head of the matter to
move out of skinny closure:
I want a pumping, palpable turgidity:
I want the condition to take on flare:
I want manifestation silk-dry:

I told this fellow:
I met him out under a soaking
elm tree:
I said you're needy:
you're so needy something's rotten:
I told him just because you have a
mailbox doesn't mean anybody has

to put anything in it:
it's your epidermal hole, nobody else's:
I was getting so much pleasure out
of soaking under the elm tree I
couldn't get interested in the guy's nasty cavity
and knew without looking I wasn't
going to put anything in there:
too bad about the elms being in dutch:

Archie:
    Summer Session has agreed (somewhat
reluctantly) to split 303 into 2
sections, with one for Baxter. I
haven't been able to reconfirm with Bax
that he does still want a second course
but I've gone ahead as if he did, with
the understanding that *someone* will
teach the plus-23 students and do so
at the same time (8:00) as you.
                                    Barry

seeing in a green yard a sailboat for sale:
worth a morning:
when you consider life
adds up
to exactly nothing:

one day I'm
going to go
out & conjure
the clouds down:
I'm going to try the cape on:

if they don't
come right down
flubbing their responsive damp bellies over the
ambience
I'm going to strip and shit:

as a writing teacher I tell them
revise the world:
they clip, trim, slice:
they bring it in:
oh no I say you've just put it on
stilts:
they lob, twist, crack:
oh no I say when they bring it in
you've killed it:
reconceive:
they bring in something new:
what's the use, I throw up my hands,
we're already two or three worlds
behind:

down this drain, endless
ingestion, getting
bloated with world: anybody toss
an old memo in: it's squirting
milk into treeping squabs:
burning's going on down
there:
the whole world's a few flakes:
it's sedimentation through seas:
those in the heights need

substantial bottoms: need the
sense
things are leveling off: hate
wide, especially open, disparities:

equilibrium fills holes with hills:

feed in a grocery list, somebody:
feed in how to fix a
telescope on, say, a comet: feed in a
few large pieces of legislation,
couple committee reports, some lab
notes, triptickets, sailing schedules,
the dawns & dusks of planets,
contemplations of squirrels:

somewhere along the line the computer
is going to perpetrate a large announcement:
then we'll know why the
imagination's
winding no scraps up into
windy transfigurations:
in our day
comfort is sunrise at 5:25:

couple systems analysts: bushel of
female ticks, engorged: some dirty
rats:
cutworms:
nightfeeders that dusk arouses:
cubic mile of infestation,
corruption, rust, pus, pus

caterpillars,
snot:
tank of wound weepage:
boxcar of love salt,
fill, siftings, winnowings, dregs,
curds, chips,
aerosols of eagerness, dozen black
widows:
a league of universal ivy stone:
choice:
much testament of need: 400
singing horses, a flask of
wart-juice from the udders of the awry:

families with a lot of living to do:
should get turquoise, shaded coppertone,
or spanish avocado:
features for fun-loving families:

discover for yourselves where
the problems are & amass
alternative strategies:
otherwise it's D– & no pussy:

Archie:
    Thanks very
much. That's a
real pleasure.
            Neil

I scribble, baby, I mean
I breeze on:

every mile a twist, I
should be back:
a smidgen slit of silence lets all
in:
the land's turning tables
greased with the finest silence
money can buy, still, the wind, mine & its,
rattles over the ridges, splits
the cords of wood & gristle:
to a cartographer
part of Pennsylvania's a broken record:
curving grooves & ridges in
visual music:

day after day the camels of the rain
bear their gray way by: the ditches
bend green grass in:
but then drought enlarges in rapids
the incidence of rocks:
but then flood, so salient, though
with muscle swirls, could
scrape you across a single
prominence,
splitting possibility like a paper shell:
it is, even after an 8-day rain,
hard to know what to ask for:
a baby robin's been out on the
lawn all day, all day wet and for
many days wet though only one
day out: maybe if it were
dry he could get to a low branch at

least, some force from those fumbling
wings, airier dry:

here are the 18-year-old
seedbeds & the
19-year-old fertilizers:
they have come for a summer session:
knowledge is to be my insemination:
I grant it them as one grants flesh
the large white needle:
what shall I tell those who are
nervous,
too tender for needles, the
splitting of iridescent tendons:
oh I tell them nothing can realize
them, nothing ruin them
like the poundage of pure self:
with my trivia
I'll dispense dignity, a sense of office,
formality they can define themselves against:
the head is my sphere:
I'll look significant as I deal with
mere wires of light, ghosts of
cells, working there.